Volleyball is Fun For Everyone

By Kandia Shorey and Kamal Martindale

Dedication

I want to dedicate this book to "The late Patrick Oxley." Thank you for the many years and starting Kamal on his volleyball journey. Continue to rest in Peace.

Hello, My name is Kamal.

Today I am going to play volleyball.

I cannot wait to see my coach.

He is so much fun.

His name is Coach Patrick.

Coach Patrick taught me how to bump, volley and spike.

I like to spike and volley.

But my favorite part of volleyball, is when I bump the ball and roll over on the ground.

Rolling on the ground is
so much fun.

My mom laughs at me
every time.

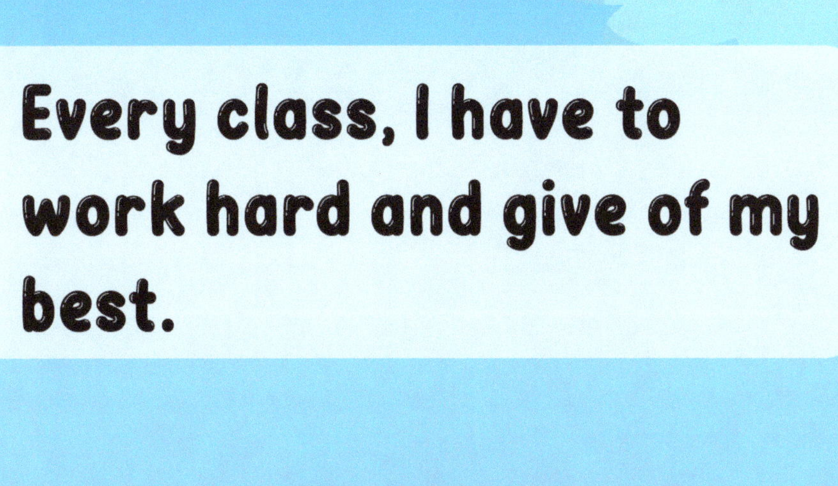
Every class, I have to work hard and give of my best.

At the end of each class, I play against Coach Patrick.

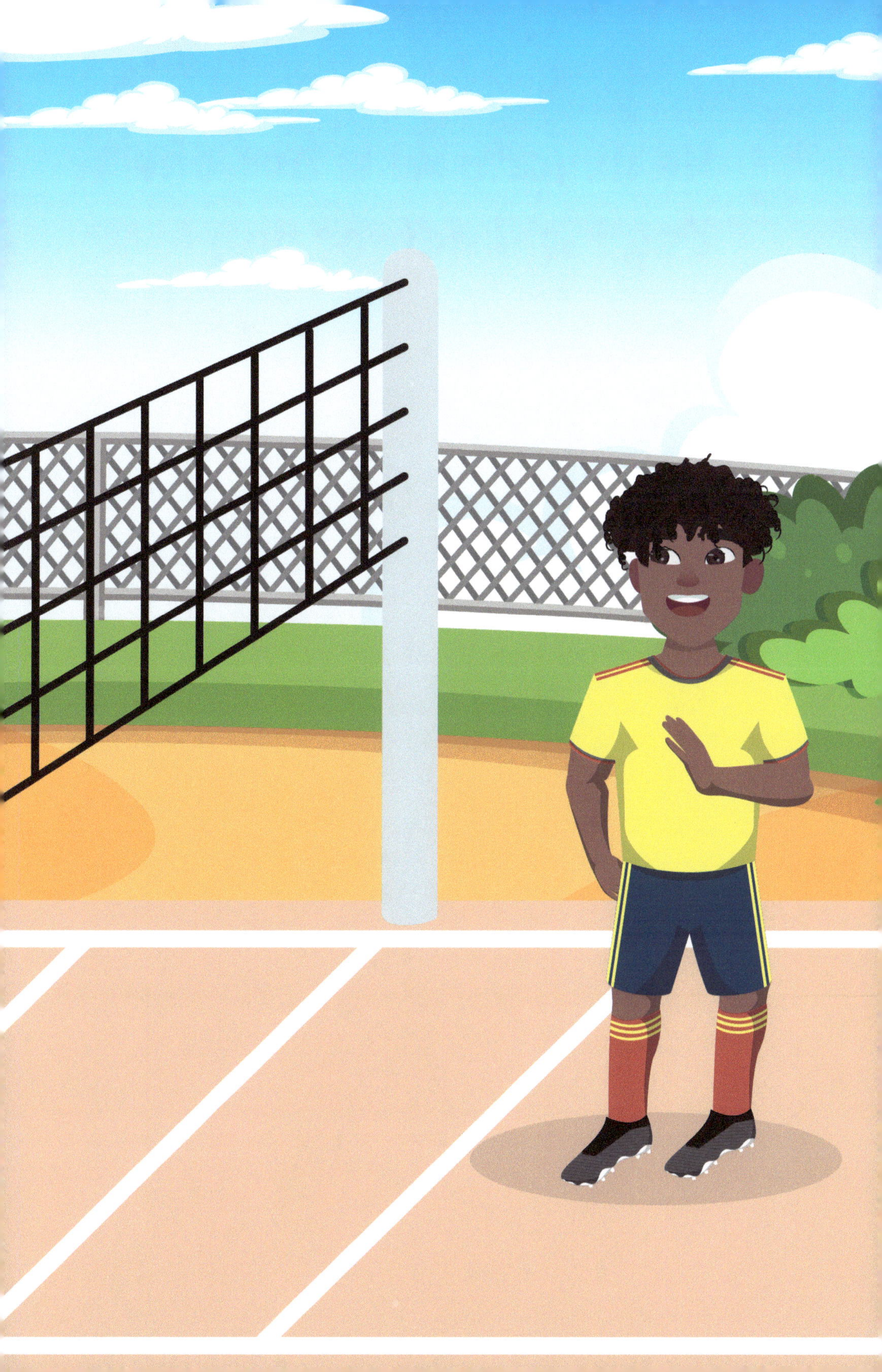

He usually wins but one day I will defeat him.

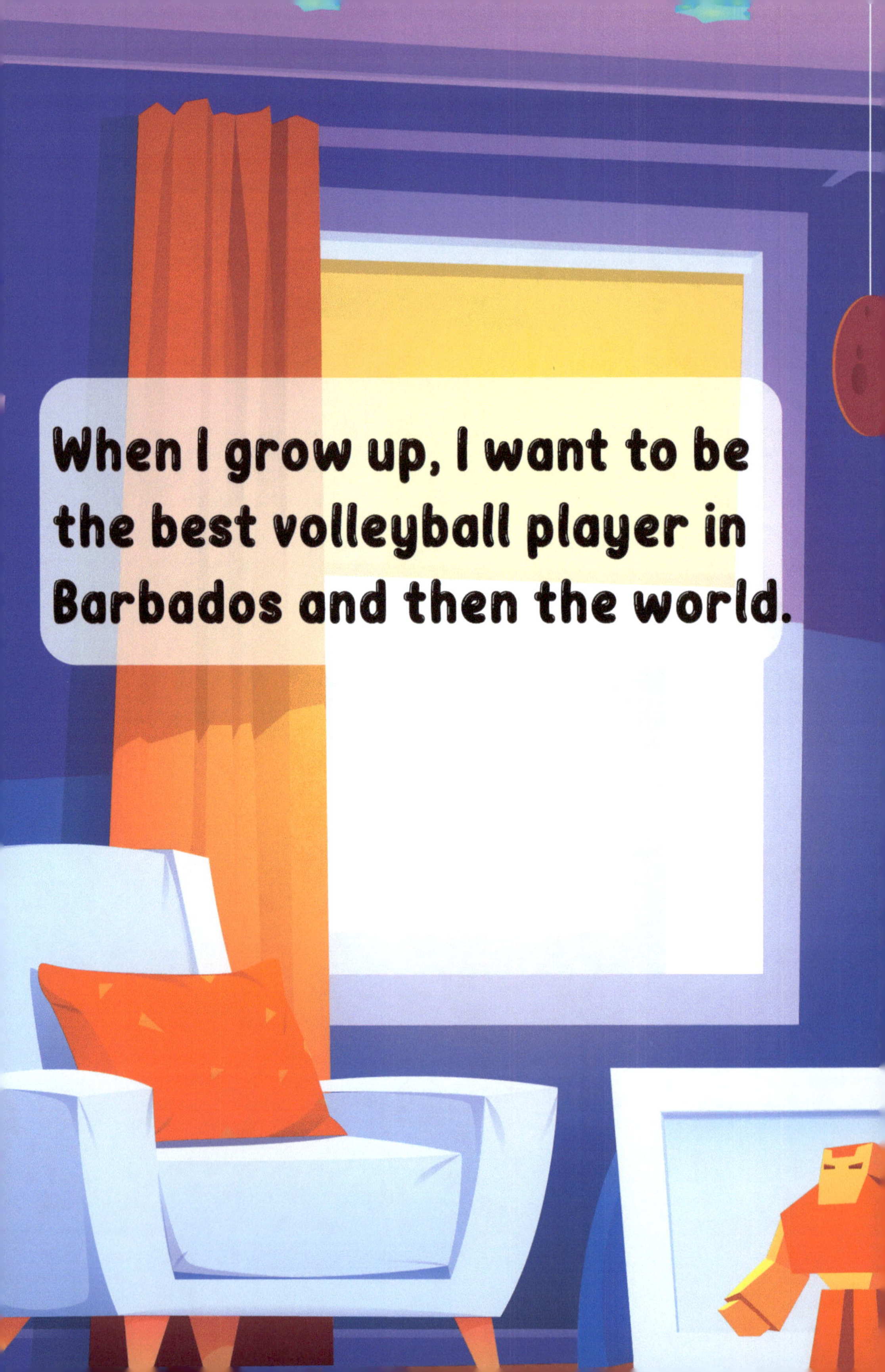

When I grow up, I want to be the best volleyball player in Barbados and then the world.

The End

About the Author

Kamal and Kandia are a mother and son duo from the island of Barbados. We are also sports enthusiasts and we want to share our island sporting experiences with the world.